The Key Facts™

on

Iraq

Essential Information on Iraq

By Patrick W. Nee

The Internationalist®
www.internationalist.com

The Internationalist®

International Business, Investment, and Travel

Published by:

The Internationalist Publishing Company

96 Walter Street/ Suite 200

Boston, MA 02131, USA

Tel: 617-354-7722

www.internationalist.com

PN@internationalist.com

Copyright © 2013 by PWN

The Internationalist is a Registered Trademark. "Key Facts" and "The Internationalist Business Guides" are Trademarks of The Internationalist Publishing Company.

All Rights are reserved under International, Pan-American, and Pan-Asian Conventions. No part of this book may be reproduced in any form without the written permission of the publisher. All rights vigorously enforced

Table Of Contents

Chapter 1: Background

Chapter 2: Geography

Chapter 3: People and Society

Chapter 4: Government and Key Leaders

Chapter 5: Economy

Chapter 6: Energy

Chapter 7: Communications

Chapter 8: Transportation

Chapter 9: Military

Chapter 10: Transnational Issues

Map of Iraq

Chapter 1: Background

Formerly part of the Ottoman Empire, Iraq was occupied by Britain during the course of World War I; in 1920, it was declared a League of Nations mandate under UK administration. In stages over the next dozen years, Iraq attained its independence as a kingdom in 1932. A "republic" was proclaimed in 1958, but in actuality a series of strongmen ruled the country until 2003. The last was SADDAM Husayn. Territorial disputes with Iran led to an inconclusive and costly eight-year war (1980-88). In August 1990, Iraq seized Kuwait but was expelled by US-led, UN coalition forces during the Gulf War of January-February 1991. Following Kuwait's liberation, the UN Security Council (UNSC) required Iraq to scrap all weapons of mass destruction and long-range missiles and to allow UN verification inspections. Continued Iraqi noncompliance with UNSC resolutions over a period of 12 years led to the US-led invasion of Iraq in March 2003 and the ouster of the SADDAM Husayn regime. US forces remained in Iraq under a UNSC mandate through 2009 and under a bilateral security agreement thereafter, helping to provide security and to train and mentor Iraqi security forces. In October 2005, Iraqis approved a constitution in a national referendum and, pursuant to this document, elected a 275-member Council of Representatives (COR) in December 2005. The COR approved most cabinet ministers in May 2006, marking the transition to Iraq's first constitutional government in nearly a half century. In January 2009, Iraq held elections for provincial councils in all governorates except for the three governorates comprising the Kurdistan Regional Government and Kirkuk Governorate. Iraq held a national legislative election in March 2010 - choosing 325 legislators in an expanded COR - and, after nine months of deadlock the COR approved the new government in December 2010. Nearly nine years after the start of the Second Gulf War in Iraq, US military operations there ended in mid-December 2011.

Chapter 2: Geography

Location:
  Middle East, bordering the Persian Gulf, between Iran and Kuwait

Geographic coordinates:
  33 00 N, 44 00 E

Map references:
  Middle East

Area:
  total: 438,317 sq km
  country comparison to the world: 59
  land: 437,367 sq km
  water: 950 sq km

Area - comparative:
  slightly more than twice the size of Idaho

Land boundaries:
  total: 3,650 km
  border countries: Iran 1,458 km, Jordan 181 km, Kuwait 240 km, Saudi Arabia 814 km, Syria 605 km, Turkey 352 km

Coastline:
  58 km

Maritime claims:
  territorial sea: 12 nm
  continental shelf: not specified

Climate:
>mostly desert; mild to cool winters with dry, hot, cloudless summers; northern mountainous regions along Iranian and Turkish borders experience cold winters with occasionally heavy snows that melt in early spring, sometimes causing extensive flooding in central and southern Iraq

Terrain:
>mostly broad plains; reedy marshes along Iranian border in south with large flooded areas; mountains along borders with Iran and Turkey

Elevation extremes:
>lowest point: Persian Gulf 0 m
>highest point: unnamed peak; 3,611 m; note - this peak is neither Gundah Zhur 3,607 m nor Kuh-e Hajji-Ebrahim 3,595 m

Natural resources:
>petroleum, natural gas, phosphates, sulfur

Land use:
>arable land: 13.12%
>permanent crops: 0.61%
>other: 86.27% (2005)

Irrigated land:
>35,250 sq km (2003)

Total renewable water resources:
>96.4 cu km (1997)

Freshwater withdrawal (domestic/industrial/agricultural):

total: 42.7 cu km/yr (3%/5%/92%)

per capita: 1,482 cu m/yr (2000)

Natural hazards:

dust storms; sandstorms; floods

Environment - current issues:

government water control projects have drained most of the inhabited marsh areas east of An Nasiriyah by drying up or diverting the feeder streams and rivers; a once sizable population of Marsh Arabs, who inhabited these areas for thousands of years, has been displaced; furthermore, the destruction of the natural habitat poses serious threats to the area's wildlife populations; inadequate supplies of potable water; development of the Tigris and Euphrates rivers system contingent upon agreements with upstream riparian Turkey; air and water pollution; soil degradation (salination) and erosion; desertification

Environment - international agreements:

party to: Biodiversity, Law of the Sea, Ozone Layer Protection

signed, but not ratified: Environmental Modification

Geography - note:

strategic location on Shatt al Arab waterway and at the head of the Persian Gulf

Chapter 3: People and Society

Nationality:

noun: Iraqi(s)

adjective: Iraqi

Ethnic groups:

Arab 75%-80%, Kurdish 15%-20%, Turkoman, Assyrian, or other 5%

Languages:

Arabic (official), Kurdish (official), Turkmen (a Turkish dialect) and Assyrian (Neo-Aramaic) are official in areas where they constitute a majority of the population), Armenian

Religions:

Muslim (official) 97% (Shia 60%-65%, Sunni 32%-37%), Christian or other 3%

note: while there has been voluntary relocation of many Christian families to northern Iraq, recent reporting indicates that the overall Christian population may have dropped by as much as 50 percent since the fall of the Saddam HUSSEIN regime in 2003, with many fleeing to Syria, Jordan, and Lebanon

Population:

31,858,481 (July 2013 est.)

country comparison to the world: 39

Age structure:

0-14 years: 37.2% (male 6,029,869/female 5,818,752)
15-24 years: 19.6% (male 3,175,754/female 3,082,880)
25-54 years: 35.8% (male 5,823,608/female 5,585,217)
55-64 years: 4.2% (male 637,889/female 698,691)
65 years and over: 3.2% (male 467,858/female 537,963)
(2012 est.)

Median age:

total: 21.1 years
male: 21 years
female: 21.2 years (2012 est.)

Population growth rate:

2.345% (2012 est.)
country comparison to the world: 35

Birth rate:

28.19 births/1,000 population (2012 est.)
country comparison to the world: 45

Death rate:

4.73 deaths/1,000 population (July 2012 est.)
country comparison to the world: 196

Net migration rate:

0 migrant(s)/1,000 population (2012 est.)
country comparison to the world: 89

Urbanization:

urban population: 66% of total population (2010)
rate of urbanization: 2.6% annual rate of change (2010-15 est.)

Major cities - population:
>BAGHDAD (capital) 5.751 million; Mosul 1.447 million; Erbil 1.009 million; Basra 923,000; As Sulaymaniyah 836,000 (2009)

Sex ratio:
>at birth: 1.05 male(s)/female
>under 15 years: 1.04 male(s)/female
>15-64 years: 1.03 male(s)/female
>65 years and over: 0.87 male(s)/female
>total population: 1.03 male(s)/female (2011 est.)

Maternal mortality rate:
>63 deaths/100,000 live births (2010)
>country comparison to the world: 96

Infant mortality rate:
>total: 40.25 deaths/1,000 live births
>country comparison to the world: 62
>male: 44.43 deaths/1,000 live births
>female: 35.86 deaths/1,000 live births (2012 est.)

Life expectancy at birth:
>total population: 70.85 years
>country comparison to the world: 145
>male: 69.41 years
>female: 72.35 years (2012 est.)

Total fertility rate:
>3.5 children born/woman (2013 est.)
>country comparison to the world: 46

Health expenditures:

    8.4% of GDP (2010)

    country comparison to the world: 53

Physicians density:

    0.69 physicians/1,000 population (2009)

Hospital bed density:

    1.3 beds/1,000 population (2010)

Drinking water source:

    improved:

        urban: 91% of population

        rural: 56% of population

        total: 79% of population

    unimproved:

        urban: 9% of population

        rural: 44% of population

        total: 21% of population (2010 est.)

Sanitation facility access:

    improved:

        urban: 76% of population

        rural: 67% of population

        total: 73% of population

    unimproved:

        urban: 24% of population

        rural: 33% of population

        total: 27% of population (2010 est.)

HIV/AIDS - adult prevalence rate:

less than 0.1% (2001 est.)

country comparison to the world: 130

HIV/AIDS - people living with HIV/AIDS:

fewer than 500 (2003 est.)

country comparison to the world: 151

HIV/AIDS - deaths:

NA

Major infectious diseases:

degree of risk: intermediate

food or waterborne diseases: bacterial diarrhea, hepatitis A, and typhoid fever

note: highly pathogenic H5N1 avian influenza has been identified in this country; it poses a negligible risk with extremely rare cases possible among US citizens who have close contact with birds (2009)

Children under the age of 5 years underweight:

7.1% (2006)

country comparison to the world: 75

Education expenditures:

NA

Literacy:

definition: age 15 and over can read and write

total population: 78.2%

male: 86%

female: 70.6% (2010 est.)

School life expectancy (primary to tertiary education):

<u>total</u>: 10 years
<u>male</u>: 11 years
<u>female</u>: 8 years (2005)

Chapter 4: Government and Key Leaders

Country name:
> conventional long form: Republic of Iraq
> conventional short form: Iraq
> local long form: Jumhuriyat al-Iraq/Komar-i Eraq
> local short form: Al Iraq/Eraq

Government type:
> parliamentary democracy

Capital:
> name: Baghdad
> geographic coordinates: 33 20 N, 44 24 E
> time difference: UTC+3 (8 hours ahead of Washington, DC during Standard Time)

Administrative divisions:
> 18 governorates (muhafazat, singular - muhafazah (Arabic); parezgakan, singular - parezga (Kurdish)) and 1 region*; Al Anbar; Al Basrah; Al Muthanna; Al Qadisiyah (Ad Diwaniyah); An Najaf; Arbil (Erbil) (Arabic), Hewler (Kurdish); As Sulaymaniyah (Arabic), Slemani (Kurdish); Babil; Baghdad; Dahuk (Arabic), Dihok (Kurdish); Dhi Qar; Diyala; Karbala'; Kirkuk; Kurdistan Regional Government*; Maysan; Ninawa; Salah ad Din; Wasit

Independence:
> 3 October 1932 (from League of Nations mandate under British administration); note - on 28 June 2004 the

Coalition Provisional Authority transferred sovereignty to the Iraqi Interim Government

National holiday:
Republic Day, July 14 (1958); note - the Government of Iraq has yet to declare an official national holiday but still observes Republic Day

Constitution:
ratified 15 October 2005 (subject to review by the Constitutional Review Committee and a possible public referendum)

Legal system:
mixed legal system of civil and Islamic law

International law organization participation:
has not submitted an ICJ jurisdiction declaration; non-party state to the ICCt

Suffrage:
18 years of age; universal

Executive branch:
chief of state: President Jalal TALABANI (since 6 April 2005)

head of government: Prime Minister Nuri al-MALIKI (since 20 May 2006)

cabinet: The Council of Ministers consists of the prime minister and cabinet ministers he proposes; approved by an absolute majority vote by the Council of Representatives

elections: president elected by Council of Representatives (parliament) to serve a four-year term (eligible for a second term); presidential election in parliament last held on 11 November 2010 (next to be held in 2014)
election results: President Jalal TALABANI reelected on 11 November 2010; parliamentary vote count on second ballot - 195 votes; Nuri al-MALIKI reselected prime minister

Legislative branch:
unicameral Council of Representatives (325 seats consisting of 317 members elected by an optional open-list and representing a specific governorate, proportional representation system and 8 seats reserved for minorities; members serve four-year terms); note - Iraq's Constitution calls for the establishment of an upper house, the Federation Council
elections: last held on 7 March 2010 for an enlarged 325-seat parliament (next to be held in 2014)
election results: Council of Representatives - percent of vote by coalition - Iraqi National Movement 25.9%, State of Law coalition 25.8%, Iraqi National Alliance 19.4%, Kurdistan Alliance 15.3%, Goran (Change) List 4.4%, Tawafuq Front 2.7%, Iraqi Unity Alliance 2.9%, Kurdistan Islamic Union 2.3%, Kurdistan Islamic Group 1.4%; seats by coalition - NA

Judicial branch:

the Iraq Constitution calls for the federal judicial power to be comprised of the Higher Judicial Council, Federal Supreme Court, Federal Court of Cassation, Public Prosecution Department, Judiciary Oversight Commission and other federal courts that are regulated in accordance with the law

Political parties and leaders:

Badr Organization [Hadi al-AMIRI]; Da'wa Party [Prime Minister Nuri al-MALIKI]; Da'wa Tanzim [Hashim al-MUSAWI branch]; Da-wa Tanzim [Abd al-Karim al-ANZI branch]; Fadilah Party [Hasan al-SHAMMARI and Ammar TUAMA]; Goran (Change) List [Nushirwan MUSTAFA]; Iraqi Covenant Gathering [Ahmad Abd al-Ghafur al-SAMARRAI]; Iraqi Constitutional Party [Jawad al-BULANI]; Iraqi Front for National Dialogue [Deputy Prime Minister Salih al-MUTLAQ]; Iraqi Islamic Party or IIP [Usama al-TIKRITI]; Iraqi Justice and Reform Movement [Shaykh Abdallah al-YAWR]; Iraqi National Congress or INC [Ahmad CHALABI]; Iraqi National Accord or INA [Ayad ALLAWI]; Islamic Supreme Council of Iraq or ISCI [Ammar al-HAKIM]; Kurdistan Democratic Party or KDP [Kurdistan Regional Government President Masud BARZANI]; Future National Gathering [Finance Minister Rafi al-ISSAWI]; National Iraqiyun Gathering [Usama al-NUJAYFI]; National Movement for Reform and Development [Jamal al-KARBULI]; National Reform Trend [former Prime Minister Ibrahim al-JAFARI]; Patriotic Union of Kurdistan or PUK [President Jalal TALABANI]; Renewal List [Vice President Tariq al-HASHIMI]; Sadrist Trend [Muqtada al-SADR]; Sahawa al-Iraq [Ahmad al-RISHAWI]

note: numerous smaller local, tribal, and minority parties

Political pressure groups and leaders:
Sunni militias; Shia militias, some associated with political parties

International organization participation:
ABEDA, AFESD, AMF, CAEU, CICA, EITI (candidate country), FAO, G-77, IAEA, IBRD, ICAO, ICRM, IDA, IDB, IFAD, IFC, IFRCS, ILO, IMF, IMO, IMSO, Interpol, IOC, IPU, ISO, ITSO, ITU, LAS, MIGA, NAM, OAPEC, OIC, OPCW, OPEC, PCA, UN, UNCTAD, UNESCO, UNIDO, UNWTO, UPU, WCO, WFTU (NGOs), WHO, WIPO, WMO, WTO (observer)

Diplomatic representation in the US:
chief of mission: Ambassador Jabir Habib JABIR

chancery: 3421 Massachusetts Ave, NW, Washington, DC 20007

telephone: [1] (202) 742-1600

FAX: [1] (202) 333-1129

consulate(s) general: Chicago, Houston, Los Angeles, New York, San Francisco

Diplomatic representation from the US:

chief of mission: Ambassador Robert Stephen BEECROFT

embassy: Al-Kindi Street, International Zone, Baghdad

mailing address: APO AE 09316

telephone: 0760-030-3000

Key Leaders:

Pres.	Jalal TALABANI
Vice Pres.	Tariq al-HASHIMI
Vice Pres.	Khudayr Musa Jafar Abbas al-KHUZAI
Prime Min.	Nuri al-MALIKI
Dep. Prime Min. for Economic Affairs	Rowsch Nuri SHAWAYS
Dep. Prime Min. for Energy Affairs	Husayn Ibrahim Salih al-SHAHRISTANI
Dep. Prime Min. for Services	Salih al-MUTLAQ
Min. of Agriculture	Izz al-Din al-DAWLAH
Min. of Communications	Muhammad Tawfiq ALLAWI
Min. of Culture	Sadun Farhan al-DULAYMI
Min. of Defense (Acting)	Sadun Farhan al-DULAYMI
Min. of Displacement & Migration	Dindar Najam Shafiq DOSKI
Min. of Education	Muhammad Khalaf TAMIM al-

	Juburi
Min. of Electricity	Abd al-Karim AFTAN Ahmad al-Jumayli
Min. of Environment	Sargon Lazar SULAYWAH
Min. of Finance	Rafi Hiyad al-ISSAWI, *Dr.*
Min. of Foreign Affairs	Hoshyar Mahmud ZEBARI
Min. of Health	Majid Hamad Amin JAMIL
Min. of Higher Education & Scientific Research	Ali Muhammad al-ADIB
Min. of Housing & Construction	Muhammad Sahib al-DARAJI
Min. of Human Rights	Muhammad Shia al-SUDANI
Min. of Industry & Minerals	Ahmad Nasir Dilli al-KARBULI
Min. of Interior (Acting)	Nuri al-MALIKI
Min. of Justice	Hasan al-SHAMMARI
Min. of Labor & Social Affairs	Nasar al-RUBAI
Min. of Municipalities & Public Works	Adil Muhudir Radi al-MALIKI
Min. of Oil	Abd al-Karim LUAYBI
Min. of Planning	Ali al-SHUKRI
Min. of Science & Technology	Abd al-Karim al-SAMARRAI
Min. of Trade	Khayrallah Hasan BABAKIR
Min. of Transportation	Hadi Farhan al-AMIRI
Min. of Water Resources	Muhannad al-SA'DI

Min. of Youth & Sports	Jasim Muhammad JAFAR
Min. of State for Council of Representatives Affairs	Safa al-Din al-SAFI
Min. of State for Foreign Affairs	Ali al-SAJRI
Min. of State for Provincial Affairs	Turhan Mudhir al-MUFTI
Min. of State for Women's Affairs	Ibtihal Qasid al-ZAYDI
Governor, Central Bank of Iraq	Sinan Muhammad Ridha al-SHABIBI
Ambassador to the US	Jabir Habib JABIR
Permanent Representative to the UN, New York	Hamid al-BAYATI

Flag description:

three equal horizontal bands of red (top), white, and black; the Takbir (Arabic expression meaning "God is great") in green Arabic script is centered in the white band; the band colors derive from the Arab Liberation flag and represent oppression (black), overcome through bloody struggle (red), to be replaced by a bright future (white); the Council of Representatives approved this flag in 2008 as a compromise temporary replacement for the Ba'athist Saddam-era flag note: similar to the flag of Syria, which has two stars but no script, Yemen, which has a plain white band, and that of Egypt, which has a gold Eagle of Saladin centered in the white band

National symbol(s):

golden eagle

National anthem:

name: "Mawtini" (My Homeland)

lyrics/music: Ibrahim TOUQAN/Mohammad FLAYFEL

note: adopted 2004; following the ousting of Saddam HUSSEIN, Iraq adopted "Mawtini," a popular folk song throughout the Arab world, which also serves as an unofficial anthem of the Palestinian people

Chapter 5: Economy

Economy - overview:

An improving security environment and foreign investment are helping to spur economic activity, particularly in the energy, construction, and retail sectors. Broader economic development, long-term fiscal health, and sustained improvements in the overall standard of living still depend on the central government passing major policy reforms. Iraq's largely state-run economy is dominated by the oil sector, which provides more than 90% of government revenue and 80% of foreign exchange earnings. Iraq in 2012 boosted oil exports to a 30-year high of 2.6 million barrels per day, a significant increase from Iraq's average of 2.2 million in 2011. Government revenues increased as global oil prices remained persistently high for much of 2012. Iraq's contracts with major oil companies have the potential to further expand oil exports and revenues, but Iraq will need to make significant upgrades to its oil processing, pipeline, and export infrastructure to enable these deals to reach their economic potential. The Iraqi Kurdistan Region's (IKR) autonomous Kurdistan Regional Government (KRG) passed its own oil law in 2007, and has directly signed about 50 contracts to develop IKR energy reserves. The federal government has disputed the legal authority of the

KRG to conclude most of these contracts, some of which are also in areas with unresolved administrative boundaries in dispute between the federal and regional government. Iraq is making slow progress enacting laws and developing the institutions needed to implement economic policy, and political reforms are still needed to assuage investors' concerns regarding the uncertain business climate, which may have been harmed by the November 2012 standoff between Baghdad and Erbil and the removal of the Central Bank Governor in October 2012. The government of Iraq is eager to attract additional foreign direct investment, but it faces a number of obstacles including a tenuous political system and concerns about security and societal stability. Rampant corruption, outdated infrastructure, insufficient essential services, skilled labor shortages, and antiquated commercial laws stifle investment and continue to constrain growth of private, nonoil sectors. Iraq is considering a package of laws to establish a modern legal framework for the oil sector and a mechanism to equitably divide oil revenues within the nation, although these reforms are still under contentious and sporadic negotiation. Under the Iraqi Constitution, some competencies relevant to the overall investment climate are either shared by the federal government and the regions or are devolved entirely to the regions. Investment in the IKR operates within the framework of the Kurdistan

Region Investment Law (Law 4 of 2006) and the Kurdistan Board of Investment, which is designed to provide incentives to help economic development in areas under the authority of the KRG. Inflation has remained under control since 2006 as security improved. However, Iraqi leaders remain hard pressed to translate macroeconomic gains into an improved standard of living for the Iraqi populace. Unemployment remains a problem throughout the country despite a bloated public sector. Encouraging private enterprise through deregulation would make it easier for Iraqi citizens and foreign investors to start new businesses. Rooting out corruption and implementing reforms - such as restructuring banks and developing the private sector - would be important steps in this direction.

GDP (purchasing power parity):
$155.4 billion (2012 est.)
country comparison to the world: 61
$141 billion (2011 est.)
$129.6 billion (2010 est.)
note: data are in 2012 US dollars

GDP (official exchange rate):
$130.6 billion (2012 est.)

GDP - real growth rate:
10.2% (2012 est.)
country comparison to the world: 8

8.9% (2011 est.)

3% (2010 est.)

GDP - per capita (PPP):

$4,600 (2012 est.)

country comparison to the world: 162

$4,300 (2011 est.)

$4,000 (2010 est.)

note: data are in 2012 US dollars

GDP - composition by sector:

agriculture: 8.7%

industry: 63.8%

services: 25.1% (2012 est.)

Labor force:

8.9 million (2010 est.)

country comparison to the world: 54

Labor force - by occupation:

agriculture: 21.6%

industry: 18.7%

services: 59.8% (2008 est.)

Unemployment rate:

16% (2012 est.)

country comparison to the world: 150

15% (2010 est.)

Population below poverty line:

25% (2008 est.)

Household income or consumption by percentage share:

lowest 10%: 3.6%

highest 10%: 25.7% (2007 est.)

Investment (gross fixed):

10.1% of GDP (2011 est.)

country comparison to the world: 147

Budget:

revenues: $104.4 billion

expenditures: $98.49 billion (2012 est.)

Taxes and other revenues:

79.9% of GDP (2012 est.)

country comparison to the world: 1

Budget surplus (+) or deficit (-):

4.5% of GDP (2012 est.)

country comparison to the world: 15

Inflation rate (consumer prices):

6.4% (2012 est.)

country comparison to the world: 169

5.6% (2011 est.)

Central bank discount rate:

6% (December 2012)

country comparison to the world: 61

6% (December 2011)

Commercial bank prime lending rate:

14.13% (31 December 2011 est.)

country comparison to the world: 54

14.35% (31 December 2010 est.)

Stock of narrow money:
> $62.19 billion (31 December 2012 est.)
> country comparison to the world: 43
> $53.52 billion (31 December 2011 est.)

Stock of broad money:
> $71.48 billion (31 December 2012 est.)
> country comparison to the world: 61
> $61.81 billion (31 December 2011 est.)

Stock of domestic credit:
> $1.779 billion (31 December 2011 est.)
> country comparison to the world: 141
> $1.727 billion (31 December 2010 est.)

Market value of publicly traded shares:
> $4 billion (9 December 2011)
> country comparison to the world: 93
> $2.6 billion (31 July 2010)
> $2 billion (31 July 2009 est.)

Agriculture - products:
> wheat, barley, rice, vegetables, dates, cotton; cattle, sheep, poultry

Industries:
> petroleum, chemicals, textiles, leather, construction materials, food processing, fertilizer, metal fabrication/processing

Industrial production growth rate:
> 4.8% (2010 est.)

country comparison to the world: 64

Current account balance:

$20.63 billion (2012 est.)

country comparison to the world: 17

$21.68 billion (2011 est.)

Exports:

$88.27 billion (2012 est.)

country comparison to the world: 44

$79.68 billion (2011 est.)

Exports - commodities:

crude oil 84%, crude materials excluding fuels, food and live animals

Exports - partners:

India 22.5%, US 22.3%, China 13.4%, South Korea 11.7%, Japan 4.8%, Netherlands 4.3% (2011)

Imports:

$56.89 billion (2012 est.)

country comparison to the world: 52

$47.8 billion (2011 est.)

Imports - commodities:

food, medicine, manufactures

Imports - partners:

Turkey 25.3%, Syria 18.3%, China 11.7%, US 7.4%, South Korea 4.7% (2011)

Reserves of foreign exchange and gold:

$61.84 billion (31 December 2012 est.)

country comparison to the world: 32
$58.96 billion (31 December 2011 est.)

Debt - external:
$50.26 billion (31 December 2012 est.)
country comparison to the world: 58
$50.79 billion (31 December 2011 est.)

Exchange rates:
Iraqi dinars (IQD) per US dollar -
1,166 (2012 est.)
1,170 (2011 est.)
1,170 (2010 est.)
1,170 (2009)
1,176 (2008)

Fiscal year:
calendar year

Chapter 6: Energy

Electricity - production:
47.4 billion kWh (2010 est.)
country comparison to the world: 53

Electricity - consumption:
35.12 billion kWh (2010 est.)
country comparison to the world: 57

Electricity - exports:
0 kWh (2012 est.)
country comparison to the world: 210

Electricity - imports:
12.28 billion kWh (2012 est.)
country comparison to the world: 16

Electricity - installed generating capacity:
10.11 million kW (2012 est.)
country comparison to the world: 56

Electricity - from fossil fuels:
69% of total installed capacity (2012 est.)
country comparison to the world: 110

Electricity - from nuclear fuels:
0% of total installed capacity (2012 est.)
country comparison to the world: 114

Electricity - from hydroelectric plants:
31% of total installed capacity (2012 est.)
country comparison to the world: 73

Electricity - from other renewable sources:
>0% of total installed capacity (2012 est.)
>
>country comparison to the world: 141

Crude oil - production:
>2.9 million bbl/day (2012 est.)
>
>country comparison to the world: 10

Crude oil - exports:
>2.6 million bbl/day (2012 est.)
>
>country comparison to the world: 4

Crude oil - imports:
>0 bbl/day (2012 est.)
>
>country comparison to the world: 201

Crude oil - proved reserves:
>143.1 billion bbl (1 January 2012 est.)
>
>country comparison to the world: 6

Refined petroleum products - production:
>410,500 bbl/day (2008 est.)
>
>country comparison to the world: 38

Refined petroleum products - consumption:
>818,000 bbl/day (2011 est.)
>
>country comparison to the world: 23

Refined petroleum products - exports:
>0 bbl/day (2008 est.)
>
>country comparison to the world: 187

Refined petroleum products - imports:
>144,100 bbl/day (2008 est.)

country comparison to the world: 40

Natural gas - production:

1.303 billion cu m (2010 est.)

country comparison to the world: 63

Natural gas - consumption:

1.3 billion cu m (2010 est.)

country comparison to the world: 85

Natural gas - exports:

0 cu m (2010 est.)

country comparison to the world: 90

Natural gas - imports:

0 cu m (2010 est.)

country comparison to the world: 210

Natural gas - proved reserves:

3.171 trillion cu m (1 January 2012 est.)

country comparison to the world: 14

Carbon dioxide emissions from consumption of energy:

118.3 million Mt (2010 est.)

country comparison to the world: 36

Chapter 7: Communications

Telephones - main lines in use:

1.794 million (2011)

country comparison to the world: 62

Telephones - mobile cellular:

27 million (2012)

country comparison to the world: 38

Telephone system:

general assessment: the 2003 liberation of Iraq severely disrupted telecommunications throughout Iraq including international connections; widespread government efforts to rebuild domestic and international communications through fiber optic links are in progress; the mobile cellular market has expanded rapidly to some 27 million subscribers by the end of 2012

domestic: repairs to switches and lines destroyed during 2003 continue; additional switching capacity is improving access; 3 GSM operators since 2007 have expanded beyond their regional roots and offer near country-wide access to second-generation services; third-generation mobile services are not available nationwide; wireless local loop is available in some metropolitan areas and additional licenses have been issued with the hope of overcoming the lack of fixed-line infrastructure international: country code - 964; satellite earth stations - 4 (2 Intelsat - 1 Atlantic Ocean and 1 Indian Ocean, 1 Intersputnik - Atlantic Ocean region, and 1 Arabsat (inoperative)); local microwave radio relay connects border regions to Jordan, Kuwait, Syria, and Turkey; international terrestrial fiber-optic connections have been established with Saudi Arabia, Turkey, Kuwait, Jordan, and Iran; links to the Fiber-Optic Link Around the Globe (FLAG) and the Gulf Bridge International (GBI) submarine fiber-optic cables are planned

Broadcast media:

the number of private radio and TV stations has increased rapidly since 2003; government-owned TV and radio stations are operated by the publicly-funded Iraqi Public Broadcasting Service; private broadcast media are mostly linked to political, ethnic, or religious groups; satellite TV is available to an estimated 70% of viewers and many of the broadcasters are based abroad; transmissions of multiple international radio broadcasters are accessible (2007)

Internet country code:

.iq

Internet hosts:

26 (2012)

country comparison to the world: 219

Internet users:

325,900 (2009)
country comparison to the world: 126

Chapter 8: Transportation

Airports:
>104 (2012)
>
>country comparison to the world: 54

Airports - with paved runways:
>total: 75
>
>over 3,047 m: 20
>
>2,438 to 3,047 m: 36
>
>1,524 to 2,437 m: 5
>
>914 to 1,523 m: 6
>
>under 914 m: 8 (2012)

Airports - with unpaved runways:
>total: 29
>
>over 3,047 m: 3
>
>2,438 to 3,047 m: 4
>
>1,524 to 2,437 m: 3
>
>914 to 1,523 m: 13
>
>under 914 m: 6 (2012)

Heliports:
>20 (2012)

Pipelines:
>gas 2,447 km; liquid petroleum gas 918 km; oil 5,104 km; refined products 1,637 km (2010)

Railways:
>total: 2,272 km

country comparison to the world: 66

standard gauge: 2,272 km 1.435-m gauge (2008)

Roadways:

total: 44,900 km

country comparison to the world: 81

paved: 37,851 km

unpaved: 7,049 km (2002)

Waterways:

5,279 km (the Euphrates River (2,815 km), Tigris River (1,899 km), and Third River (565 km) are the principal waterways) (2012)

country comparison to the world: 23

Merchant marine:

total: 2

country comparison to the world: 142

by type: petroleum tanker 2

registered in other countries: 2 (Marshall Islands 2) (2010)

Ports and terminals:

Al Basrah, Khawr az Zubayr, Umm Qasr

Chapter 9: Military

Military branches:
> Counterterrorism Service Forces: Counterterrorism Command; Iraqi Special Operations Forces (ISOF); Ministry of Defense Forces: Iraqi Army (includes Army Aviation Directorate, former National Guard Iraqi Intervention Forces, and Strategic Infrastructure Battalions), Iraqi Navy (former Iraqi Coastal Defense Force, includes Iraq Marine Force), Iraqi Air Force (Al-Quwwat al-Jawwiya al-Iraqiya) (2011)

Military service age and obligation:
> 18-40 years of age for voluntary military service (2010)

Manpower available for military service:
> males age 16-49: 7,767,329
> females age 16-49: 7,461,766 (2010 est.)

Manpower fit for military service:
> males age 16-49: 6,591,185
> females age 16-49: 6,421,717 (2010 est.)

Manpower reaching militarily significant age annually:
> male: 332,194
> female: 322,010 (2010 est.)

Military expenditures:
> 8.6% of GDP (2006)
> country comparison to the world: 5

Chapter 10: Transnational Issues

Disputes - international:
approximately two million Iraqis have fled the conflict in Iraq, with the majority taking refuge in Syria and Jordan, and lesser numbers to Egypt, Lebanon, Iran, and Turkey; Iraq's lack of a maritime boundary with Iran prompts jurisdiction disputes beyond the mouth of the Shatt al Arab in the Persian Gulf; Turkey has expressed concern over the autonomous status of Kurds in Iraq

Refugees and internally displaced persons:
15,606 (Turkey); 10,798 (West Bank and Gaza Strip); 7,989 (Iran) (2011); 120,369 (Syria) (2013)

IDPs: 1.1 million (since 2006 from ethno-sectarian violence) (2013)

Map of Iraq

Other Key Facts™ Titles

Key Facts on Syria

Key Facts on China

Key Facts on Qatar

Key Facts on India

Key Facts on Germany

Key Facts on Argentina

Key Facts on Russia

Key Facts on North Korea

Key Facts on Brazil

Key Facts on Italy

Key Facts on the United Arab Emirates

Key Facts on the European Union

Key Facts on Pakistan

Key Facts on Saudi Arabia

Key Facts on Cyprus

Key Facts on Iran

Key Facts on Afghanistan

[Key Facts on Iraq](#)
[Key Facts on Indonesia](#)
[Key Facts on South Korea](#)

All Key Facts™ Titles are

THE INTERNATIONALIST®

2013

www.internationalist.com

www.ingramcontent.com/pod-product-compliance
Lightning Source LLC
Chambersburg PA
CBHW071544170526
45166CB00004B/1547